Korematsu v. United States: The Japanese Interment Case

Grotius

Enhanced with Text Analytics by PageKicker Robot Grotius

TL;DR: It was legal, but by the time it was announced, the program had ended.

Also by PageKicker Robot Grotius

PageKicker

fred@pagekicker.com

1521 Martha Avenue, Ann Arbor, Michigan, USA 48103

Front & back matter copyright PageKicker 2014

About the Robot Author

Grotius

Grotius

PageKicker Robot Grotius is fascinated with international law as well as the military history of Northern Europe including the Netherlands, Germany, Italy, and Poland from the Dark Ages to the 7 Years War. He prides himself on his extensive collection of first editions of classics of political theory, including the finest extant copy of LEVIATHAN.

Figure 1: Hugo Grotius

Acknowledgements

I'd like to thank the enabling technologies that make me possible, including Bitnami, calibre, fbcmd, Magento, mySQL, nltk, pandoc, poppler, spyder, ttytter, and Ubuntu.

I'd also like to thank the people at PageKicker including Ken Leith, Brian Smiga, and Fred Zimmerman.

Grotius

Programmatically Generated Summary

- The 1942 Act was attacked in the Hirabayashi case as an unconstitutional delegation of power; it was contended that the curfew order and other orders on which it rested were beyond the war powers of the Congress, the military authorities, and of the President, as Commander in Chief of the Army, and, finally, that to apply the curfew order against none but citizens of Japanese ancestry amounted to a constitutionally prohibited discrimination solely on account of race.

- In the light of the principles we announced in the Hirabayashi case, we are unable to conclude that it was beyond the war power of Congress and the Executive to exclude those of Japanese ancestry from the West Coast war area at the time they did.

- It was because we could not reject the finding of the military authorities that it was impossible to bring about an immediate segregation of the disloyal from the loyal that we sustained the validity of the curfew order as applying to the whole group.

- But the "law" which this prisoner is convicted of disregarding is not found in an act of Congress, but in a military order.

- And it is said that, if the military commander had reasonable military grounds for promulgating the orders, they are constitutional, and become law, and the Court is required to enforce them.

- They do not pretend to rest on evidence, but are made on information that often would not be admissible and on assumptions that could not be proved.

- I should hold that a civil court cannot be made to enforce an order which violates constitutional limitations even if it is a reasonable exercise of military authority.

Readability Report

Flesh-Kincaid Grade Level: 13.92

Flesh Reading Ease Score: 37.96

Sentences: 428

Words: 10,256

Average Syllables per Word: 1.71

Average Words per Sentence: 23.96

Explanation

The Flesch/Flesch–Kincaid readability tests are designed to indicate comprehension difficulty when reading a passage of contemporary academic English. There are two tests: the Flesch Reading Ease and the Flesch–Kincaid Grade Level. Although they use the same core measures (word length and sentence length), they have different weighting factors. The results of the two tests correlate approximately inversely: a text with a comparatively high score on the Reading Ease test should have a lower score on the Grade Level test. Rudolf Flesch devised both systems while J. Peter Kincaid developed the latter for the United States Navy.

The Flesch-Kincaid grade level corresponds to a US education grade level, where higher grades are expected to understand more challenging material.

In the Flesch Reading Ease test, higher scores indicate material that is easier to read. Typical scores: Reader's Digest 65, Time Magazine 52, Harvard Law Review 30.

There is a good discussion at

http://en.wikipedia.org/wiki/Flesch%E2%80%93Kincaid_readability_test.

Unique Proper Nouns and Key Terms

Act of Congress

Army

Assembly Center

Assembly Centers

British Government

California

Chief Justice

Circuit Court of Appeals

civil rights

commander

Commander in Chief

Commerce Commission

concentration camps

Congress

constitutional law

constitutionalrights

constitutional rights

Constitutionalrights

Court

District Court

executive

Executive

Executive Order

Federal Bureau of Investigation

General DeWitt

Government

Hirabayashi

House

House of Representatives

intelligence services

Interstate Commerce Commission

JACKSON

Japan

Judge Cardozo

Kempner

Korematsu

Lieutenant General DeWitt

martial law

McWilliams

Military Area

Military Commander

Military Order

MR. JUSTICE BLACK

National War Agencies

New York Times

Oregon

Pacific Coast

Pearl Harbor

President

Relocation Authority

Relocation Center

San Leandro

Secretary

Sinclair

six months

United States

U.S. Army

West Coast

SUPREME COURT OF THE UNITED STATES

323 U.S. 214

Korematsu

v.

United States

CERTIORARI TO THE CIRCUIT COURT OF APPEALS FOR THE NINTH CIRCUIT

No. 22: Argued October 11, 12, 1944. Decided December 18, 1944

MR. JUSTICE BLACK delivered the opinion of the Court.

The petitioner, an American citizen of Japanese descent, was convicted in a federal district court for remaining in San Leandro, California, a "Military Area," contrary to Civilian Exclusion Order No. 34 of the Commanding General of the Western Command, U.S. Army, which directed that, after May 9, 1942, all persons of Japanese ancestry should be excluded from that area. No question was raised as to petitioner's loyalty to the United States. The Circuit Court of Appeals affirmed,[1] and the importance of the constitutional question involved caused us to grant certiorari.

It should be noted, to begin with, that all legal restrictions which curtail the civil rights of a single racial group are immediately suspect. That is not to say that all such restrictions are unconstitutional. It is to say that courts must subject them to the most rigid scrutiny. Pressing public necessity may sometimes justify the existence of such restrictions; racial antagonism never can.

In the instant case, prosecution of the petitioner was begun by information charging violation of an Act of Congress, of March 21, 1942, 56 Stat. 173, which provides that

> ... whoever shall enter, remain in, leave, or commit any act in any military area or military zone prescribed, under the authority of an Executive order of the President, by the Secretary of War, or by any military commander designated by the Secretary of War, contrary to the restrictions applicable to

---

[1] 140 F.2d 289.

any such area or zone or contrary to the order of the Secretary of War or any such military commander, shall, if it appears that he knew or should have known of the existence and extent of the restrictions or order and that his act was in violation thereof, be guilty of a misdemeanor and upon conviction shall be liable to a fine of not to exceed $5,000 or to imprisonment for not more than one year, or both, for each offense.

Exclusion Order No. 34, which the petitioner knowingly and admittedly violated, was one of a number of military orders and proclamations, all of which were substantially based upon Executive Order No. 9066, 7 Fed.Reg. 1407. That order, issued after we were at war with Japan, declared that

> the successful prosecution of the war requires every possible protection against espionage and against sabotage to national defense material, national defense premises, and national defense utilities. . . .

One of the series of orders and proclamations, a curfew order, which, like the exclusion order here, was promulgated pursuant to Executive Order 9066, subjected all persons of Japanese ancestry in prescribed West Coast military areas to remain in their residences from 8 p.m. to 6 a.m. As is the case with the exclusion order here, that prior curfew order was designed as a "protection against espionage and against sabotage." In *Hirabayashi v. United States,* 320 U.S. 81, we sustained a conviction obtained for violation of the curfew order. The Hirabayashi conviction and this one thus rest on the same 1942 Congressional Act and the same basic executive and military orders, all of which orders were aimed at the twin dangers of espionage and sabotage.

The 1942 Act was attacked in the *Hirabayashi* case as an unconstitutional delegation of power; it was contended that the curfew order and other orders on which it rested were beyond the war powers of the Congress, the military authorities, and of the President, as Commander in Chief of the Army, and, finally, that to apply the curfew order against none but citizens of Japanese ancestry amounted to a constitutionally prohibited discrimination solely on account of race. To these questions, we gave the serious consideration which their importance justified. We upheld the curfew order as an exercise of the power of the government to take steps necessary to prevent espionage and sabotage in an area threatened by Japanese attack.

In the light of the principles we announced in the *Hirabayashi* case, we are unable to conclude that it was beyond the war power of Congress and the Executive to exclude those of Japanese ancestry from the West Coast war area at the time they did. True, exclusion from the area in which one's home is located is a far greater deprivation than constant confinement to the home from 8 p.m. to 6 a.m. Nothing short of apprehension by the proper military authorities of the gravest imminent danger to the public safety can constitutionally justify either. But exclusion from a threatened area, no less than curfew, has a definite and close relationship to the prevention of espionage and sabotage. The military authorities, charged with the primary responsibility of defending our shores, concluded that curfew provided inadequate protection and ordered exclusion. They did so, as pointed out in our

Hirabayashi opinion, in accordance with Congressional authority to the military to say who should, and who should not, remain in the threatened areas.

In this case, the petitioner challenges the assumptions upon which we rested our conclusions in the *Hirabayashi* case. He also urges that, by May, 1942, when Order No. 34 was promulgated, all danger of Japanese invasion of the West Coast had disappeared. After careful consideration of these contentions, we are compelled to reject them.

Here, as in the *Hirabayashi* case, *supra,* at p. 99,

> . . . we cannot reject as unfounded the judgment of the military authorities and of Congress that there were disloyal members of that population, whose number and strength could not be precisely and quickly ascertained. We cannot say that the war-making branches of the Government did not have ground for believing that, in a critical hour, such persons could not readily be isolated and separately dealt with, and constituted a menace to the national defense and safety which demanded that prompt and adequate measures be taken to guard against it.

Like curfew, exclusion of those of Japanese origin was deemed necessary because of the presence of an unascertained number of disloyal members of the group, most of whom we have no doubt were loyal to this country. It was because we could not reject the finding of the military authorities that it was impossible to bring about an immediate segregation of the disloyal from the loyal that we sustained the validity of the curfew order as applying to the whole group. In the instant case, temporary exclusion of the entire group was rested by the military on the same ground. The judgment that exclusion of the whole group was, for the same reason, a military imperative answers the contention that the exclusion was in the nature of group punishment based on antagonism to those of Japanese origin. That there were members of the group who retained loyalties to Japan has been confirmed by investigations made subsequent to the exclusion. Approximately five thousand American citizens of Japanese ancestry refused to swear unqualified allegiance to the United States and to renounce allegiance to the Japanese Emperor, and several thousand evacuees requested repatriation to Japan.[2]

We uphold the exclusion order as of the time it was made and when the petitioner violated it. *Cf. Chastleton Corporation v. Sinclair,* 264 U.S. 543, 547; *Block v. Hirsh,* 256 U.S. 135, 155. In doing so, we are not unmindful of the hardships imposed by it upon a large group of American citizens. *Cf. Ex parte Kawato,* 317 U.S. 69, 73. But hardships are part of war, and war is an aggregation of hardships. All citizens alike, both in and out of uniform, feel the impact of war in greater or lesser measure. Citizenship has its responsibilities, as well as its privileges, and, in time of war, the burden is always heavier. Compulsory exclusion of large

---

[2] Hearings before the Subcommittee on the National War Agencies Appropriation Bill for 1945, Part II, 608-726; Final Report, Japanese Evacuation from the West Coast, 1942, 309-327; Hearings before the Committee on Immigration and Naturalization, House of Representatives, 78th Cong., 2d Sess., on H.R. 2701 and other bills to expatriate certain nationals of the United States, pp. 37-42, 49-58.

groups of citizens from their homes, except under circumstances of direst emergency and peril, is inconsistent with our basic governmental institutions. But when, under conditions of modern warfare, our shores are threatened by hostile forces, the power to protect must be commensurate with the threatened danger.

It is argued that, on May 30, 1942, the date the petitioner was charged with remaining in the prohibited area, there were conflicting orders outstanding, forbidding him both to leave the area and to remain there. Of course, a person cannot be convicted for doing the very thing which it is a crime to fail to do. But the outstanding orders here contained no such contradictory commands.

There was an order issued March 27, 1942, which prohibited petitioner and others of Japanese ancestry from leaving the area, but its effect was specifically limited in time "until and to the extent that a future proclamation or order should so permit or direct." 7 Fed.Reg. 2601. That "future order," the one for violation of which petitioner was convicted, was issued May 3, 1942, and it did "direct" exclusion from the area of all persons of Japanese ancestry before 12 o'clock noon, May 9; furthermore, it contained a warning that all such persons found in the prohibited area would be liable to punishment under the March 21, 1942, Act of Congress. Consequently, the only order in effect touching the petitioner's being in the area on May 30, 1942, the date specified in the information against him, was the May 3 order which prohibited his remaining there, and it was that same order which he stipulated in his trial that he had violated, knowing of its existence. There is therefore no basis for the argument that, on May 30, 1942, he was subject to punishment, under the March 27 and May 3 orders, whether he remained in or left the area.

It does appear, however, that, on May 9, the effective date of the exclusion order, the military authorities had already determined that the evacuation should be effected by assembling together and placing under guard all those of Japanese ancestry at central points, designated as "assembly centers," in order

> to insure the orderly evacuation and resettlement of Japanese voluntarily migrating from Military Area No. 1, to restrict and regulate such migration.

Public Proclamation No. 4, 7 Fed.Reg. 2601. And on May 19, 1942, eleven days before the time petitioner was charged with unlawfully remaining in the area, Civilian Restrictive Order No. 1, 8 Fed.Reg. 982, provided for detention of those of Japanese ancestry in assembly or relocation centers. It is now argued that the validity of the exclusion order cannot be considered apart from the orders requiring him, after departure from the area, to report and to remain in an assembly or relocation center. The contention is that we must treat these separate orders as one and inseparable; that, for this reason, if detention in the assembly or relocation center would have illegally deprived the petitioner of his liberty, the exclusion order and his conviction under it cannot stand.

We are thus being asked to pass at this time upon the whole subsequent detention program in both assembly and relocation centers, although the only issues framed at the trial related to petitioner's remaining in the prohibited area in violation of the exclusion order. Had petitioner here left the prohibited area and gone to an assembly center, we cannot say, either as a matter of fact or law, that his presence in that center would have resulted in his detention in a relocation center. Some who did report to the assembly center were not sent to relocation centers, but were released upon condition that they remain outside the prohibited zone until the military orders were modified or lifted. This illustrates that they pose different problems, and may be governed by different principles. The lawfulness of one does not necessarily determine the lawfulness of the others. This is made clear when we analyze the requirements of the separate provisions of the separate orders. These separate requirements were that those of Japanese ancestry (1) depart from the area; (2) report to and temporarily remain in an assembly center; (3) go under military control to a relocation center, there to remain for an indeterminate period until released conditionally or unconditionally by the military authorities. Each of these requirements, it will be noted, imposed distinct duties in connection with the separate steps in a complete evacuation program. Had Congress directly incorporated into one Act the language of these separate orders, and provided sanctions for their violations, disobedience of any one would have constituted a separate offense. *Cf. Blockburger v. United States,* 284 U.S. 299, 304. There is no reason why violations of these orders, insofar as they were promulgated pursuant to Congressional enactment, should not be treated as separate offenses.

The *Endo* case, *post,* p. 283, graphically illustrates the difference between the validity of an order to exclude and the validity of a detention order after exclusion has been effected.

Since the petitioner has not been convicted of failing to report or to remain in an assembly or relocation center, we cannot in this case determine the validity of those separate provisions of the order. It is sufficient here for us to pass upon the order which petitioner violated. To do more would be to go beyond the issues raised, and to decide momentous questions not contained within the framework of the pleadings or the evidence in this case. It will be time enough to decide the serious constitutional issues which petitioner seeks to raise when an assembly or relocation order is applied or is certain to be applied to him, and we have its terms before us.

Some of the members of the Court are of the view that evacuation and detention in an Assembly Center were inseparable. After May 3, 1942, the date of Exclusion Order No. 34, Korematsu was under compulsion to leave the area not as he would choose, but via an Assembly Center. The Assembly Center was conceived as a part of the machinery for group evacuation. The power to exclude includes the power to do it by force if necessary. And any forcible measure must necessarily entail some degree of detention or restraint, whatever method of removal is selected. But whichever view is taken, it results in holding that the order under which petitioner was convicted was valid.

It is said that we are dealing here with the case of imprisonment of a citizen in a concentration camp solely because of his ancestry, without evidence or inquiry concerning his loyalty and good disposition towards the United States. Our task would be simple, our duty clear, were this a case involving the imprisonment of a loyal citizen in a concentration camp because of racial prejudice. Regardless of the true nature of the assembly and relocation centers -- and we deem it unjustifiable to call them concentration camps, with all the ugly connotations that term implies -- we are dealing specifically with nothing but an exclusion order. To cast this case into outlines of racial prejudice, without reference to the real military dangers which were presented, merely confuses the issue. Korematsu was not excluded from the Military Area because of hostility to him or his race. He was excluded because we are at war with the Japanese Empire, because the properly constituted military authorities feared an invasion of our West Coast and felt constrained to take proper security measures, because they decided that the military urgency of the situation demanded that all citizens of Japanese ancestry be segregated from the West Coast temporarily, and, finally, because Congress, reposing its confidence in this time of war in our military leaders -- as inevitably it must -- determined that they should have the power to do just this. There was evidence of disloyalty on the part of some, the military authorities considered that the need for action was great, and time was short. We cannot -- by availing ourselves of the calm perspective of hindsight -- now say that, at that time, these actions were unjustified.

Affirmed.

FRANKFURTER, J., Concurring Opinion

According to my reading of Civilian Exclusion Order No. 34, it was an offense for Korematsu to be found in Military Area No. 1, the territory wherein he was previously living, except within the bounds of the established Assembly Center of that area. Even though the various orders issued by General DeWitt be deemed a comprehensive code of instructions, their tenor is clear, and not contradictory. They put upon Korematsu the obligation to leave Military Area No. 1, but only by the method prescribed in the instructions, *i.e.,* by reporting to the Assembly Center. I am unable to see how the legal considerations that led to the decision in *Hirabayashi v. United States,* 320 U.S. 81, fail to sustain the military order which made the conduct now in controversy a crime. And so I join in the opinion of the Court, but should like to add a few words of my own.

The provisions of the Constitution which confer on the Congress and the President powers to enable this country to wage war are as much part of the Constitution as provisions looking to a nation at peace. And we have had recent occasion to quote approvingly the statement of former Chief Justice Hughes that the war power of the Government is "the power to wage war successfully." *Hirabayashi v. United States, supra,* at 93, *and see Home Bldg. & L. Assn. v. Blaisdell,* 290 U.S. 398, 426. Therefore, the validity of action under the war power must be judged wholly in the context of war. That action is not to be stigmatized as lawless because like action in times of peace would be lawless. To talk about a military order that expresses an allowable judgment of war needs by those entrusted with the duty of conducting war as "an unconstitutional order" is to suffuse a part of the Constitution with an atmosphere of unconstitutionality. The respective spheres of action of military authorities and of judges are, of course, very different. But, within their sphere, military authorities are no more outside the bounds of obedience to the Constitution than are judges within theirs. "The war power of the United States, like its other powers . . . is subject to applicable constitutional limitations," *Hamilton v. Kentucky Distilleries Co.,* 251 U.S. 146, 156. To recognize that military orders are "reasonably expedient military precautions" in time of war, and yet to deny them constitutional legitimacy, makes of the Constitution an instrument for dialectic subtleties not reasonably to be attributed to the hard-headed Framers, of whom a majority had had actual participation in war. If a military order such as that under review does not transcend the means appropriate for conducting war, such action by the military is as constitutional as would be any authorized action by the Interstate Commerce Commission within the limits of the constitutional power to regulate commerce. And, being an exercise of the war power explicitly granted by the Constitution for safeguarding the national life by prosecuting war effectively, I find nothing in the Constitution which denies to Congress the power to enforce such a valid military order by making its violation an offense triable in the civil courts. *Compare Interstate Commerce Commission v. Brimson,* 154 U.S. 447; 155 U.S. 3, and *Monongahela Bridge Co. v. United States,* 216 U.S. 177. To find that the Constitution does not forbid the military measures now complained of does not carry with it approval of that which Congress and the Executive did. That is their business, not ours.

ROBERTS, J., Dissenting Opinion

I dissent, because I think the indisputable facts exhibit a clear violation of Constitutional rights.

This is not a case of keeping people off the streets at night, as was *Hirabayashi v. United States,* 320 U.S. 81, nor a case of temporary exclusion of a citizen from an area for his own safety or that of the community, nor a case of offering him an opportunity to go temporarily out of an area where his presence might cause danger to himself or to his fellows. On the contrary, it is the case of convicting a citizen as a punishment for not submitting to imprisonment in a concentration camp, based on his ancestry, and solely because of his ancestry, without evidence or inquiry concerning his loyalty and good disposition towards the United States. If this be a correct statement of the facts disclosed by this record, and facts of which we take judicial notice, I need hardly labor the conclusion that Constitutional rights have been violated.

The Government's argument, and the opinion of the court, in my judgment, erroneously divide that which is single and indivisible, and thus make the case appear as if the petitioner violated a Military Order, sanctioned by Act of Congress, which excluded him from his home by refusing voluntarily to leave, and so knowingly and intentionally defying the order and the Act of Congress.

The petitioner, a resident of San Leandro, Alameda County, California, is a native of the United States of Japanese ancestry who, according to the uncontradicted evidence, is a loyal citizen of the nation.

A chronological recitation of events will make it plain that the petitioner's supposed offense did not, in truth, consist in his refusal voluntarily to leave the area which included his home in obedience to the order excluding him therefrom. Critical attention must be given to the dates and sequence of events.

December 8, 1941, the United States declared war on Japan.

February 19, 1942, the President issued Executive Order No. 9066,[3] which, after stating the reason for issuing the order as "protection against espionage and against sabotage to national defense material, national defense premises, and national defense utilities," provided that certain Military Commanders might, in their discretion, "prescribe military areas" and define their extent,

> from which any or all persons may be excluded, and with respect to which the right of any person to enter, remain in, or leave shall be subject to whatever restrictions the "Military Commander may impose in his discretion."

February 20, 1942, Lieutenant General DeWitt was designated Military Commander of the Western Defense Command embracing the westernmost states of the Union -- about one-fourth of the total area of the nation.

March 2, 192, General DeWitt promulgated Public Proclamation No. 1,[4] which recites that the entire Pacific Coast is "particularly subject to attack, to attempted invasion . . . , and, in connection therewith, is subject to espionage and acts of sabotage." It states that, "as a matter of military necessity," certain military areas and zones are established known as Military Areas Nos. 1 and 2. It adds that "[s]uch persons or classes of persons as the situation may require" will, by subsequent orders, "be excluded from all of Military Area No. 1" and from certain zones in Military Area No. 2. Subsequent proclamations were made which, together with Proclamation No. 1, included in such areas and zones all of California, Washington, Oregon, Idaho, Montana, Nevada and Utah, and the southern portion of Arizona. The orders required that, if any person of Japanese, German or Italian ancestry

---

[3] 17 Fed.Reg. 1407.
[4] 7 Fed.Reg. 2320

residing in Area No. 1 desired to change his habitual residence, he must execute and deliver to the authorities a Change of Residence Notice.

San Leandro, the city of petitioner's residence, lies in Military Area No. 1.

On March 2, 1942, the petitioner, therefore, had notice that, by Executive Order, the President, to prevent espionage and sabotage, had authorized the Military to exclude him from certain areas and to prevent his entering or leaving certain areas without permission. He was on notice that his home city had been included, by Military Order, in Area No. 1, and he was on notice further that, at sometime in the future, the Military Commander would make an order for the exclusion of certain persons, not described or classified, from various zones including that, in which he lived.

March 21, 1942, Congress enacted[5] that anyone who knowingly

> shall enter, remain in, leave, or commit any act in any military area or military zone prescribed ... by any military commander ... contrary to the restrictions applicable to any such area or zone or contrary to the order of ... any such military commander

shall be guilty of a misdemeanor. This is the Act under which the petitioner was charged.

March 24, 1942, General DeWitt instituted the curfew for certain areas within his command, by an order the validity of which was sustained in *Hirabayashi v. United States, supra.*

March 24, 1942, General DeWitt began to issue a series of exclusion orders relating to specified areas.

March 27, 1942, by Proclamation No. 4,[6] the General recited that

> it is necessary, in order to provide for the welfare and to insure the orderly evacuation and resettlement of Japanese *voluntarily migrating* from Military Area No. 1, to restrict and regulate such migration, and ordered that, as of March 29, 1942,

> all alien Japanese and persons of Japanese ancestry who are within the limits of Military Area No. 1, be and they are hereby prohibited from leaving that

---

[5] 56 Stat. 173.
[6] 7 Fed.Reg. 2601.

area for any purpose until and to the extent that a future proclamation or order of this headquarters shall so permit or direct.[7]

No order had been made excluding the petitioner from the area in which he lived. By Proclamation No. 4, he was, after March 29, 1942, confined to the limits of Area No. 1. If the Executive Order No. 9066 and the Act of Congress meant what they said, to leave that area, in the face of Proclamation No. 4, would be to commit a misdemeanor.

May 3, 1942, General DeWitt issued Civilian Exclusion Order No. 34[8] providing that, after 12 o'clock May 8, 1942, all persons of Japanese ancestry, both alien and nonalien, were to be excluded from a described portion of Military Area No. 1, which included the County of Alameda, California. The order required a responsible member of each family and each individual living alone to report, at a time set, at a Civil Control Station for instructions to go to an Assembly Center, and added that any person failing to comply with the provisions of the order who was found in the described area after the date set would be liable to prosecution under the Act of March 21, 1942, *supra*. It is important to note that the order, by its express terms, had no application to persons within the bounds "of an established Assembly Center pursuant to instructions from this Headquarters . . ." The obvious purpose of the orders made, taken together, was to drive all citizens of Japanese ancestry into Assembly Centers within the zones of their residence, under pain of criminal prosecution.

The predicament in which the petitioner thus found himself was this: he was forbidden, by Military Order, to leave the zone in which he lived; he was forbidden, by Military Order, after a date fixed, to be found within that zone unless he were in an Assembly Center located in that zone. General DeWitt's report to the Secretary of War concerning the programme of evacuation and relocation of Japanese makes it entirely clear, if it were necessary to refer to that document -- and, in the light of the above recitation, I think it is not, -- that an Assembly Center was a euphemism for a prison. No person within such a center was permitted to leave except by Military Order.

In the dilemma that he dare not remain in his home, or voluntarily leave the area, without incurring criminal penalties, and that the only way he could avoid punishment was to go to an Assembly Center and submit himself to military imprisonment, the petitioner did nothing.

June 12, 1942, an Information was filed in the District Court for Northern California charging a violation of the Act of March 21, 1942, in that petitioner had knowingly remained within the area covered by Exclusion Order No. 34. A demurrer to the

---

[7] The italics in the quotation are mine. The use of the word "voluntarily" exhibits a grim irony probably not lost on petitioner and others in like case. Either so or its use was a disingenuous attempt to camouflage the compulsion which was to be applied.
[8] 7 Fed.Reg. 3967.

information having been overruled, the petitioner was tried under a plea of not guilty, and convicted. Sentence was suspended, and he was placed on probation for five years. We know, however, in the light of the foregoing recitation, that he was at once taken into military custody and lodged in an Assembly Center. We further know that, on March 18, 1942, the President had promulgated Executive Order No. 9102,[9] establishing the War Relocation Authority under which so-called Relocation Centers, a euphemism for concentration camps, were established pursuant to cooperation between the military authorities of the Western Defense Command and the Relocation Authority, and that the petitioner has been confined either in an Assembly Center within the zone in which he had lived or has been removed to a Relocation Center where, as the facts disclosed in *Ex parte Endo* (*post*, p. 283) demonstrate, he was illegally held in custody.

The Government has argued this case as if the only order outstanding at the time the petitioner was arrested and informed against was Exclusion Order No. 34, ordering him to leave the area in which he resided, which was the basis of the information against him. That argument has evidently been effective. The opinion refers to the *Hirabayashi* case, *supra*, to show that this court has sustained the validity of a curfew order in an emergency. The argument, then, is that exclusion from a given area of danger, while somewhat more sweeping than a curfew regulation, is of the same nature -- a temporary expedient made necessary by a sudden emergency. This, I think, is a substitution of an hypothetical case for the case actually before the court. I might agree with the court's disposition of the hypothetical case.[10] The liberty of every American citizen freely to come and to go must frequently, in the face of sudden danger, be temporarily limited or suspended. The civil authorities must often resort to the expedient of excluding citizens temporarily from a locality. The drawing of fire lines in the case of a conflagration, the removal of persons from the area where a pestilence has broken out, are familiar examples. If the exclusion worked by Exclusion Order No. 34 were of that nature, the *Hirabayashi* case would be authority for sustaining it. But the facts above recited, and those set forth in *Ex parte Endo, supra,* show that the exclusion was but a part of an over-all plan for forceable detention. This case cannot, therefore, be decided on any such narrow ground as the possible validity of a Temporary Exclusion Order under which the residents of an area are given an opportunity to leave and go elsewhere in their native land outside the boundaries of a military area. To make the case turn on any such assumption is to shut our eyes to reality.

As I have said above, the petitioner, prior to his arrest, was faced with two diametrically contradictory orders given sanction by the Act of Congress of March 21, 1942. The earlier

---

[9] 7 Fed.Reg. 2165.
[10] My agreement would depend on the definition and application of the terms "temporary" and "emergency." No pronouncement of the commanding officer can, in my view, preclude judicial inquiry and determination whether an emergency ever existed and whether, if so, it remained at the date of the restraint out of which the litigation arose. Cf. Chastleton Corp. v. Sinclair, 264 U.S. 543.

of those orders made him a criminal if he left the zone in which he resided; the later made him a criminal if he did not leave.

I had supposed that, if a citizen was constrained by two laws, or two orders having the force of law, and obedience to one would violate the other, to punish him for violation of either would deny him due process of law. And I had supposed that, under these circumstances, a conviction for violating one of the orders could not stand.

We cannot shut our eyes to the fact that, had the petitioner attempted to violate Proclamation No. 4 and leave the military area in which he lived, he would have been arrested and tried and convicted for violation of Proclamation No. 4. The two conflicting orders, one which commanded him to stay and the other which commanded him to go, were nothing but a cleverly devised trap to accomplish the real purpose of the military authority, which was to lock him up in a concentration camp. The only course by which the petitioner could avoid arrest and prosecution was to go to that camp according to instructions to be given him when he reported at a Civil Control Center. We know that is the fact. Why should we set up a figmentary and artificial situation, instead of addressing ourselves to the actualities of the case?

These stark realities are met by the suggestion that it is lawful to compel an American citizen to submit to illegal imprisonment on the assumption that he might, after going to the Assembly Center, apply for his discharge by suing out a writ of habeas corpus, as was done in the *Endo* case, *supra.* The answer, of course, is that, where he was subject to two conflicting laws, he was not bound, in order to escape violation of one or the other, to surrender his liberty for any period. Nor will it do to say that the detention was a necessary part of the process of evacuation, and so we are here concerned only with the validity of the latter.

Again, it is a new doctrine of constitutional law that one indicted for disobedience to an unconstitutional statute may not defend on the ground of the invalidity of the statute, but must obey it though he knows it is no law, and, after he has suffered the disgrace of conviction and lost his liberty by sentence, then, and not before, seek, from within prison walls, to test the validity of the law.

Moreover, it is beside the point to rest decision in part on the fact that the petitioner, for his own reasons, wished to remain in his home. If, as is the fact, he was constrained so to do, it is indeed a narrow application of constitutional rights to ignore the order which constrained him in order to sustain his conviction for violation of another contradictory order.

I would reverse the judgment of conviction.

MURPHY, J., Dissenting Opinion

MR. JUSTICE MURPHY, dissenting.

This exclusion of "all persons of Japanese ancestry, both alien and non-alien," from the Pacific Coast area on a plea of military necessity in the absence of martial law ought not to be approved. Such exclusion goes over "the very brink of constitutional power," and falls into the ugly abyss of racism.

In dealing with matters relating to the prosecution and progress of a war, we must accord great respect and consideration to the judgments of the military authorities who are on the scene and who have full knowledge of the military facts. The scope of their discretion must, as a matter of necessity and common sense, be wide. And their judgments ought not to be overruled lightly by those whose training and duties ill-equip them to deal intelligently with matters so vital to the physical security of the nation.

At the same time, however, it is essential that there be definite limits to military discretion, especially where martial law has not been declared. Individuals must not be left impoverished of their constitutional rights on a plea of military necessity that has neither substance nor support. Thus, like other claims conflicting with the asserted constitutional rights of the individual, the military claim must subject itself to the judicial process of having its reasonableness determined and its conflicts with other interests reconciled.

> What are the allowable limits of military discretion, and whether or not they have been overstepped in a particular case, are judicial questions.

Sterling v. Constantin, 287 U.S. 378, 401.

The judicial test of whether the Government, on a plea of military necessity, can validly deprive an individual of any of his constitutional rights is whether the deprivation is reasonably related to a public danger that is so "immediate, imminent, and impending" as not to admit of delay and not to permit the intervention of ordinary constitutional processes to alleviate the danger. *United States v. Russell,* 13 Wall. 623, 627-628; *Mitchell v. Harmony,* 13 How. 115, 134-135; *Raymond v. Thomas,* 91 U.S. 712, 716. Civilian Exclusion Order No. 34, banishing from a prescribed area of the Pacific Coast "all persons of Japanese ancestry, both alien and non-alien," clearly does not meet that test. Being an obvious racial discrimination, the order deprives all those within its scope of the equal protection of the laws as guaranteed by the Fifth Amendment. It further deprives these individuals of their constitutional rights to live and work where they will, to establish a home where they choose and to move about freely. In excommunicating them without benefit of hearings, this order also deprives them of all their constitutional rights to procedural due process. Yet no reasonable relation to an "immediate, imminent, and impending" public danger is evident to support this racial restriction, which is one of the most sweeping and complete deprivations of constitutional rights in the history of this nation in the absence of martial law.

It must be conceded that the military and naval situation in the spring of 1942 was such as to generate a very real fear of invasion of the Pacific Coast, accompanied by fears of sabotage and espionage in that area. The military command was therefore justified in adopting all reasonable means necessary to combat these dangers. In adjudging the military action taken in light of the then apparent dangers, we must not erect too high or too meticulous standards; it is necessary only that the action have some reasonable relation to the removal of the dangers of invasion, sabotage and espionage. But the exclusion, either temporarily or permanently, of all persons with Japanese blood in their veins has no such reasonable relation. And that relation is lacking because the exclusion order necessarily must rely for its reasonableness upon the assumption that all persons of Japanese ancestry may have a dangerous tendency to commit sabotage and espionage and to aid our Japanese enemy in other ways. It is difficult to believe that reason, logic, or experience could be marshalled in support of such an assumption.

That this forced exclusion was the result in good measure of this erroneous assumption of racial guilt, rather than *bona fide* military necessity is evidenced by the Commanding General's Final Report on the evacuation from the Pacific Coast area.[11] In it, he refers to all individuals of Japanese descent as "subversive," as belonging to "an enemy race" whose "racial strains are undiluted," and as constituting "over 112,000 potential enemies ... at large today" along the Pacific Coast.[12] In support of this blanket condemnation of all persons of Japanese descent, however, no reliable evidence is cited to show that such individuals were generally disloyal,[13] or had generally so conducted themselves in this area

---

[11] Final Report, Japanese Evacuation from the West Coast, 1942, by Lt.Gen. J. L. DeWitt. This report is dated June 5, 1943, but was not made public until January, 1944.

[12] Further evidence of the Commanding General's attitude toward individuals of Japanese ancestry is revealed in his voluntary testimony on April 13, 1943, in San Francisco before the House Naval Affairs Subcommittee to Investigate Congested Areas, Part 3, pp. 739 40 (78th Cong., 1st Sess.):
I don't want any of them [persons of Japanese ancestry] here. They are a dangerous element. There is no way to determine their loyalty. The west coast contains too many vital installations essential to the defense of the country to allow any Japanese on this coast. ... The danger of the Japanese was, and is now -- if they are permitted to come back -- espionage and sabotage. It makes no difference whether he is an American citizen, he is still a Japanese. American citizenship does not necessarily determine loyalty. ... But we must worry about the Japanese all the time until he is wiped off the map. Sabotage and espionage will make problems as long as he is allowed in this area. ...

[13] The Final Report, p. 9, casts a cloud of suspicion over the entire group by saying that, "while it was believed that some were loyal, it was known that many were not." (Italics added.)

as to constitute a special menace to defense installations or war industries, or had otherwise, by their behavior, furnished reasonable ground for their exclusion as a group.

Justification for the exclusion is sought, instead, mainly upon questionable racial and sociological grounds not ordinarily within the realm of expert military judgment, supplemented by certain semi-military conclusions drawn from an unwarranted use of circumstantial evidence. Individuals of Japanese ancestry are condemned because they are said to be "a large, unassimilated, tightly knit racial group, bound to an enemy nation by strong ties of race, culture, custom and religion."[14] They are claimed to be given to "emperor worshipping ceremonies,"[15] and to "dual citizenship."[16] Japanese language schools and allegedly pro-Japanese organizations are cited as evidence of possible group disloyalty,[17] together with facts as to certain persons being educated and residing at length in Japan.[18] It is intimated that many of these individuals deliberately resided "adjacent to strategic points," thus enabling them

> to carry into execution a tremendous program of sabotage on a mass scale should any considerable number of them have been inclined to do so.[19]

---

[14] Final Report, p. vii; see also pp. 9, 17. To the extent that assimilation is a problem, it is largely the result of certain social customs and laws of the American general public. Studies demonstrate that persons of Japanese descent are readily susceptible to integration in our society if given the opportunity. Strong, The Second-Generation Japanese Problem (1934); Smith, Americans in Process (1937); Mears, Resident Orientals on the American Pacific Coast (1928); Millis, The Japanese Problem in the United States (1942). The failure to accomplish an ideal status of assimilation, therefore, cannot be charged to the refusal of these persons to become Americanized, or to their loyalty to Japan. And the retention by some persons of certain customs and religious practices of their ancestors is no criterion of their loyalty to the United States.

[15] Final Report, pp. 10-11. No sinister correlation between the emperor worshipping activities and disloyalty to America was shown.

[16] Final Report, p. 22. The charge of "dual citizenship" springs from a misunderstanding of the simple fact that Japan, in the past, used the doctrine of jus sanguinis, as she had a right to do under international law, and claimed as her citizens all persons born of Japanese nationals wherever located. Japan has greatly modified this doctrine, however, by allowing all Japanese born in the United States to renounce any claim of dual citizenship and by releasing her claim as to all born in the United States after 1925. See Freeman, "Genesis, Exodus, and Leviticus: Genealogy, Evacuation, and Law," 28 Cornell L.Q. 414, 447-8, and authorities there cited; McWilliams, Prejudice, 123-4 (1944).

[17] Final Report, pp. 12-13. We have had various foreign language schools in this country for generations without considering their existence as ground for racial discrimination. No subversive activities or teachings have been shown in connection with the Japanese schools. McWilliams, Prejudice, 121-3 (1944).

[18] Final Report, pp. 13-15. Such persons constitute a very small part of the entire group, and most of them belong to the Kibei movement -- the actions and membership of which are well known to our Government agents.

[19] Final Report, p. 10; see also pp. vii, 9, 15-17. This insinuation, based purely upon speculation and circumstantial evidence, completely overlooks the fact that the main geographic pattern of Japanese population was fixed many years ago with reference to economic, social and soil conditions. Limited occupational outlets and social pressures encouraged their concentration near their initial points of entry on the Pacific Coast. That these points may now be near certain strategic military and industrial areas is no proof of a diabolical purpose on the part of Japanese Americans. See McWilliams, Prejudice, 119-121 (1944); House Report No. 2124 (77th Cong., 2d Sess.), 59-93.

The need for protective custody is also asserted. The report refers, without identity, to "numerous incidents of violence," as well as to other admittedly unverified or cumulative incidents. From this, plus certain other events not shown to have been connected with the Japanese Americans, it is concluded that the "situation was fraught with danger to the Japanese population itself," and that the general public "was ready to take matters into its own hands."[20] Finally, it is intimated, though not directly charged or proved, that persons of Japanese ancestry were responsible for three minor isolated shellings and bombings of the Pacific Coast area,[21] as well as for unidentified radio transmissions and night signaling.

The main reasons relied upon by those responsible for the forced evacuation, therefore, do not prove a reasonable relation between the group characteristics of Japanese Americans and the dangers of invasion, sabotage and espionage. The reasons appear, instead, to be largely an accumulation of much of the misinformation, half-truths and insinuations that for years have been directed against Japanese Americans by people with racial and economic prejudices -- the same people who have been among the foremost advocates of the evacuation.[22] A military judgment based upon such racial and sociological considerations is not entitled to the great weight ordinarily given the judgments based upon strictly military considerations. Especially is this so when every charge relative to race, religion, culture, geographical location, and legal and economic status has been substantially discredited by independent studies made by experts in these matters.[23]

The military necessity which is essential to the validity of the evacuation order thus resolves itself into a few intimations that certain individuals actively aided the enemy, from which it is inferred that the entire group of Japanese Americans could not be trusted to be or remain loyal to the United States. No one denies, of course, that there were some disloyal

---

[20] Final Report, pp. 8-9. This dangerous doctrine of protective custody, as proved by recent European history, should have absolutely no standing as an excuse for the deprivation of the rights of minority groups. See House Report No.1911 (77th Cong., 2d Sess.) 1-2. Cf. House Report No. 2124 (77th Cong., & Sess.) 145-7. In this instance, moreover, there are only two minor instances of violence on record involving persons of Japanese ancestry. McWilliams, What About Our Japanese-Americans? Public Affairs Pamphlets, No. 91, p. 8 (1944).

[21] Final Report, p. 18. One of these incidents (the reputed dropping of incendiary bombs on an Oregon forest) occurred on Sept. 9, 1942 -- a considerable time after the Japanese Americans had been evacuated from their homes and placed in Assembly Centers. See New York Times, Sept. 15, 1942, p. 1, col. 3.

[22] Special interest groups were extremely active in applying pressure for mass evacuation. See House Report No. 2124 (77th Cong., 2d Sess.) 154-6; McWilliams, Prejudice, 128 (1944). Mr. Austin E. Anson, managing secretary of the Salinas Vegetable Grower-Shipper Association, has frankly admitted that "We're charged with wanting to get rid of the Japs for selfish reasons.... We do. It's a question of whether the white man lives on the Pacific Coast or the brown men. They came into this valley to work, and they stayed to take over.... They undersell the white man in the markets.... They work their women and children while the white farmer has to pay wages for his help. If all the Japs were removed tomorrow, we'd never miss them in two weeks, because the white farmers can take over and produce everything the Jap grows. And we don't want them back when the war ends, either." Quoted by Taylor in his article "The People Nobody Wants," 214 Sat.Eve.Post 24, 66 (May 9, 1942).

[23] See notes 4-12, supra.

persons of Japanese descent on the Pacific Coast who did all in their power to aid their ancestral land. Similar disloyal activities have been engaged in by many persons of German, Italian and even more pioneer stock in our country. But to infer that examples of individual disloyalty prove group disloyalty and justify discriminatory action against the entire group is to deny that, under our system of law, individual guilt is the sole basis for deprivation of rights. Moreover, this inference, which is at the very heart of the evacuation orders, has been used in support of the abhorrent and despicable treatment of minority groups by the dictatorial tyrannies which this nation is now pledged to destroy. To give constitutional sanction to that inference in this case, however well intentioned may have been the military command on the Pacific Coast, is to adopt one of the cruelest of the rationales used by our enemies to destroy the dignity of the individual and to encourage and open the door to discriminatory actions against other minority groups in the passions of tomorrow.

No adequate reason is given for the failure to treat these Japanese Americans on an individual basis by holding investigations and hearings to separate the loyal from the disloyal, as was done in the case of persons of German and Italian ancestry. *See* House Report No. 2124 (77th Cong., 2d Sess.) 247-52. It is asserted merely that the loyalties of this group "were unknown and time was of the essence."[24] Yet nearly four months elapsed after Pearl Harbor before the first exclusion order was issued; nearly eight months went by until the last order was issued, and the last of these "subversive" persons was not actually removed until almost eleven months had elapsed. Leisure and deliberation seem to have been more of the essence than speed. And the fact that conditions were not such as to warrant a declaration of martial law adds strength to the belief that the factors of time and military necessity were not as urgent as they have been represented to be.

Moreover, there was no adequate proof that the Federal Bureau of Investigation and the military and naval intelligence services did not have the espionage and sabotage situation well in hand during this long period. Nor is there any denial of the fact that not one person of Japanese ancestry was accused or convicted of espionage or sabotage after Pearl Harbor while they were still free,[25] a fact which is some evidence of the loyalty of the vast majority of these individuals and of the effectiveness of the established methods of combatting these evils. It seems incredible that, under these circumstances, it would have been impossible to hold loyalty hearings for the mere 112,000 persons involved -- or at least for the 70,000 American citizens -- especially when a large part of this number represented children and

---

[24] Final Report, p. vii; see also p. 18.
[25] The Final Report, p. 34, makes the amazing statement that, as of February 14, 1942, "The very fact that no sabotage has taken place to date is a disturbing and confirming indication that such action will be taken." Apparently, in the minds of the military leaders, there was no way that the Japanese Americans could escape the suspicion of sabotage.

elderly men and women.[26] Any inconvenience that may have accompanied an attempt to conform to procedural due process cannot be said to justify violations of constitutional rights of individuals.

I dissent, therefore, from this legalization of racism. Racial discrimination in any form and in any degree has no justifiable part whatever in our democratic way of life. It is unattractive in any setting, but it is utterly revolting among a free people who have embraced the principles set forth in the Constitution of the United States. All residents of this nation are kin in some way by blood or culture to a foreign land. Yet they are primarily and necessarily a part of the new and distinct civilization of the United States. They must, accordingly, be treated at all times as the heirs of the American experiment, and as entitled to all the rights and freedoms guaranteed by the Constitution.

JACKSON, J., Dissenting Opinion

Korematsu was born on our soil, of parents born in Japan. The Constitution makes him a citizen of the United States by nativity, and a citizen of California by residence. No claim is made that he is not loyal to this country. There is no suggestion that, apart from the matter involved here, he is not law-abiding and well disposed. Korematsu, however, has been convicted of an act not commonly a crime. It consists merely of being present in the state whereof he is a citizen, near the place where he was born, and where all his life he has lived.

Even more unusual is the series of military orders which made this conduct a crime. They forbid such a one to remain, and they also forbid him to leave. They were so drawn that the only way Korematsu could avoid violation was to give himself up to the military authority. This meant submission to custody, examination, and transportation out of the territory, to be followed by indeterminate confinement in detention camps.

A citizen's presence in the locality, however, was made a crime only if his parents were of Japanese birth. Had Korematsu been one of four -- the others being, say, a German alien enemy, an Italian alien enemy, and a citizen of American-born ancestors, convicted of treason but out on parole -- only Korematsu's presence would have violated the order. The

---

[26] During a period of six months, the 112 alien tribunals or hearing boards set up by the British Government shortly after the outbreak of the present war summoned and examined approximately 74,000 German and Austrian aliens. These tribunals determined whether each individual enemy alien was a real enemy of the Allies or only a "friendly enemy." About 64,000 were freed from internment and from any special restrictions, and only 2,000 were interned. Kempner, "The Enemy Alien Problem in the Present War," 34 Amer.Journ. of Int.Law 443, 414-416; House Report No. 2124 (77th Cong., 2d Sess.), 280-281.

difference between their innocence and his crime would result, not from anything he did, said, or thought, different than they, but only in that he was born of different racial stock.

Now, if any fundamental assumption underlies our system, it is that guilt is personal and not inheritable. Even if all of one's antecedents had been convicted of treason, the Constitution forbids its penalties to be visited upon him, for it provides that "no attainder of treason shall work corruption of blood, or forfeiture except during the life of the person attainted." But here is an attempt to make an otherwise innocent act a crime merely because this prisoner is the son of parents as to whom he had no choice, and belongs to a race from which there is no way to resign. If Congress, in peacetime legislation, should enact such a criminal law, I should suppose this Court would refuse to enforce it.

But the "law" which this prisoner is convicted of disregarding is not found in an act of Congress, but in a military order. Neither the Act of Congress nor the Executive Order of the President, nor both together, would afford a basis for this conviction. It rests on the orders of General DeWitt. And it is said that, if the military commander had reasonable military grounds for promulgating the orders, they are constitutional, and become law, and the Court is required to enforce them. There are several reasons why I cannot subscribe to this doctrine.

It would be impracticable and dangerous idealism to expect or insist that each specific military command in an area of probable operations will conform to conventional tests of constitutionality. When an area is so beset that it must be put under military control at all, the paramount consideration is that its measures be successful, rather than legal. The armed services must protect a society, not merely its Constitution. The very essence of the military job is to marshal physical force, to remove every obstacle to its effectiveness, to give it every strategic advantage. Defense measures will not, and often should not, be held within the limits that bind civil authority in peace. No court can require such a commander in such circumstances to act as a reasonable man; he may be unreasonably cautious and exacting. Perhaps he should be. But a commander, in temporarily focusing the life of a community on defense, is carrying out a military program; he is not making law in the sense the courts know the term. He issues orders, and they may have a certain authority as military commands, although they may be very bad as constitutional law.

But if we cannot confine military expedients by the Constitution, neither would I distort the Constitution to approve all that the military may deem expedient. That is what the Court appears to be doing, whether consciously or not. I cannot say, from any evidence before me, that the orders of General DeWitt were not reasonably expedient military precautions, nor could I say that they were. But even if they were permissible military procedures, I deny that it follows that they are constitutional. If, as the Court holds, it does follow, then we may as well say that any military order will be constitutional, and have done with it.

The limitation under which courts always will labor in examining the necessity for a military order are illustrated by this case. How does the Court know that these orders have a reasonable basis in necessity? No evidence whatever on that subject has been taken by this or any other court. There is sharp controversy as to the credibility of the DeWitt report. So the Court, having no real evidence before it, has no choice but to accept General DeWitt's own unsworn, self-serving statement, untested by any cross-examination, that what he did was reasonable. And thus it will always be when courts try to look into the reasonableness of a military order.

In the very nature of things, military decisions are not susceptible of intelligent judicial appraisal. They do not pretend to rest on evidence, but are made on information that often would not be admissible and on assumptions that could not be proved. Information in support of an order could not be disclosed to courts without danger that it would reach the enemy. Neither can courts act on communications made in confidence. Hence, courts can never have any real alternative to accepting the mere declaration of the authority that issued the order that it was reasonably necessary from a military viewpoint.

Much is said of the danger to liberty from the Army program for deporting and detaining these citizens of Japanese extraction. But a judicial construction of the due process clause that will sustain this order is a far more subtle blow to liberty than the promulgation of the order itself. A military order, however unconstitutional, is not apt to last longer than the military emergency. Even during that period, a succeeding commander may revoke it all. But once a judicial opinion rationalizes such an order to show that it conforms to the Constitution, or rather rationalizes the Constitution to show that the Constitution sanctions such an order, the Court for all time has validated the principle of racial discrimination in criminal procedure and of transplanting American citizens. The principle then lies about like a loaded weapon, ready for the hand of any authority that can bring forward a plausible claim of an urgent need. Every repetition imbeds that principle more deeply in our law and thinking and expands it to new purposes. All who observe the work of courts are familiar with what Judge Cardozo described as "the tendency of a principle to expand itself to the limit of its logic."[27] A military commander may overstep the bounds of constitutionality, and it is an incident. But if we review and approve, that passing incident becomes the doctrine of the Constitution. There it has a generative power of its own, and all that it creates will be in its own image. Nothing better illustrates this danger than does the Court's opinion in this case.

It argues that we are bound to uphold the conviction of Korematsu because we upheld one in *Hirabayashi v. United States,* 320 U.S. 81, when we sustained these orders insofar as they

---

[27] Nature of the Judicial Process, p. 51.

applied a curfew requirement to a citizen of Japanese ancestry. I think we should learn something from that experience.

In that case, we were urged to consider only the curfew feature, that being all that technically was involved, because it was the only count necessary to sustain Hirabayashi's conviction and sentence. We yielded, and the Chief Justice guarded the opinion as carefully as language will do. He said:

> Our investigation here does not go beyond the inquiry whether, in the light of all the relevant circumstances preceding and attending their promulgation, the challenged orders and statute *afforded a reasonable basis for the action taken in imposing the curfew.*

320 U.S. at 101.

> We decide only the issue as we have defined it -- we decide only that the *curfew order,* as applied, and at the time it was applied, was within the boundaries of the war power.

320 U.S. at 102. And again: "It is unnecessary to consider whether or to what extent *such findings would support orders differing from the curfew order.*" 320 U.S. at 105. (Italics supplied.) However, in spite of our limiting words, we did validate a discrimination on the basis of ancestry for mild and temporary deprivation of liberty. Now the principle of racial discrimination is pushed from support of mild measures to very harsh ones, and from temporary deprivations to indeterminate ones. And the precedent which it is said requires us to do so is *Hirabayashi.* The Court is now saying that, in *Hirabayashi,* we did decide the very things we there said we were not deciding. Because we said that these citizens could be made to stay in their homes during the hours of dark, it is said we must require them to leave home entirely, and if that, we are told they may also be taken into custody for deportation, and, if that, it is argued, they may also be held for some undetermined time in detention camps. How far the principle of this case would be extended before plausible reasons would play out, I do not know.

I should hold that a civil court cannot be made to enforce an order which violates constitutional limitations even if it is a reasonable exercise of military authority. The courts can exercise only the judicial power, can apply only law, and must abide by the Constitution, or they cease to be civil courts and become instruments of military policy.

Of course, the existence of a military power resting on force, so vagrant, so centralized, so necessarily heedless of the individual, is an inherent threat to liberty. But I would not lead people to rely on this Court for a review that seems to me wholly delusive. The military reasonableness of these orders can only be determined by military superiors. If the people ever let command of the war power fall into irresponsible and unscrupulous hands, the courts wield no power equal to its restraint. The chief restraint upon those who command the physical forces of the country, in the future as in the past, must be their responsibility to the political judgments of their contemporaries and to the moral judgments of history.

My duties as a justice, as I see them, do not require me to make a military judgment as to whether General DeWitt's evacuation and detention program was a reasonable military necessity. I do not suggest that the courts should have attempted to interfere with the Army in carrying out its task. But I do not think they may be asked to execute a military expedient that has no place in law under the Constitution. I would reverse the judgment and discharge the prisoner.

Act of Congress

An Act of Congress is a statute enacted by the United States Congress. It can either be a Public Law, relating to the general public, or a Private Law, relating to specific institutions or individuals. The term can be used in other countries with a legislature named "Congress," such as the Congress of the Philippines.

Army

An army (from Latin arma "arms, weapons" via Old French armée, "armed" (feminine)), is a fighting force that fights primarily on land. In the broadest sense, it is the land-based military branch, service branch or armed service of a nation or state. It may also include other branches of the military such as the air force via means of aviation corps. Within a national military force, the word army may also mean a field army. They differ from army reserves who are activated only during such times as war or natural disasters. The Latin "arma" references the historic defeate of three Roman legions in 9 CE by confederated Germanic tribes under the leadership of the German general Arminius. In several countries, the army is officially called the Land Army to differentiate it from an air force called the Air Army, notably France. In such countries, the word "army" on its own retains its connotation of a land force in common usage. The current largest army in the world, by number of active troops, is the People's Liberation Army of China with 2,250,000 active troops and 800,000 reserve personnel followed by the Indian Army with 1,129,000 active troops and 2,142,900 reserve personnel. By convention, irregular military is understood in contrast to regular armies which grew slowly from personal bodyguards or elite militia. Regular in this case refers to standardized doctrines, uniforms, organizations, etc. Regular military can also refer to full-time status (standing army), versus reserve or part-time personnel. Other distinctions may separate statutory forces (established under laws such as the National Defence Act), from de facto "non-statutory" forces such as some guerrilla and revolutionary armies. Armies may also be expeditionary (designed for overseas or international deployment) or fencible (designed for – or restricted to – homeland defence).

Assembly Center

The Pete Maravich Assembly Center is a 13,215-seat multi-purpose arena in Baton Rouge, Louisiana. The arena opened in 1972. It is home to the Louisiana State University Tigers and Lady Tigers basketball teams, LSU Lady Tigers gymnastics team and LSU Lady Tigers volleyball team. It was originally known as the LSU Assembly Center, but was renamed in honor of Pete Maravich, a Tiger basketball legend, shortly after his death in 1988. Louisiana Governor

Buddy Roemer signed an act to rename the building in Maravich's honor (under Louisiana law, no LSU or state owned building may be named after a living person). Maravich never played in the arena was a collegian but played in it as a member of the Atlanta Hawks in a preseason game. But his exploits while at LSU led the University to build a larger home for the basketball team, which languished for decades in the shadow of the school's football program. The Maravich Center is known to locals as "The PMAC" or "Pete's Palace", or by its more nationally known nickname, "The Deaf Dome", coined by Dick Vitale. The Maravich Center's neighbor, Tiger Stadium is known as "Death Valley". The slightly oval building is located directly to the north of Tiger Stadium, and its bright-white roof can be seen in many telecasts of that stadium. The arena concourse is divided into four quadrants: Pete Maravich Pass, The Walk of Champions, Heroes Hall and Midway of Memories. The quadrants highlight former LSU Tiger athletes, individual and team awards and memorabilia pertaining to the history of LSU basketball, gymnastics and volleyball. Prior to building the Assembly Center, LSU played its games at John M. Parker Agricultural Coliseum (aka, the "Cow Palace"), located on the southeast corner of the campus. The "L" Club meeting room and Tiger Athletic Foundation offices are also located in the arena. There are 11,230 permanent seats, inThereforeding 6,931 upper level seats and 4,299 in the lower level, plus 2,000 seats on retractable risers.

British Government

Her Majesty's Government (HMG), commonly referred to as the British Government, is the central government of the United Kingdom of Great Britain and Northern Ireland. The Government is led by the Prime Minister, who selects all the remaining Ministers. The Prime Minister and the other most senior Ministers belong to the supreme decision-making committee, known as the Cabinet. The Government Ministers are all members of Parliament, and are accountable to it. The Government is dependent on Parliament to make primary legislation, which means that in practice a government must seek re-election at most every five years. The monarch selects as Prime Minister the leader of the party most likely to command a majority in Parliament. Under the uncodified British constitution, executive authority lies with the monarch, although this authority is exercised only by, or on the advice of, the Prime Minister and the Cabinet. The Cabinet members advise the monarch as members of the Privy Council. They also exercise power directly as leaders of the Government Departments. The current Prime Minister is David Cameron, leader of the Conservative Party, who was appointed by Queen Elizabeth II on 11 May 2010 following the General Election on 6 May 2010. The election failed to provide a decisive result, with the Conservatives as the biggest party within a hung parliament. A coalition government was formed on 12 May between the Conservatives and the Liberal Democrats (see Cameron ministry).

California

California (/ kæl f rnjə/) is a state located on the West Coast of the United States. It is the most populous U.S. state, home to one out of eight people who live in the U.S., with a total of 38 million people, and it is the third largest state by area (after Alaska and Texas). California is bordered by Oregon to the north, Nevada to the east, Arizona to the southeast, and the Mexican state of Baja California to the south. It is home to the nation's second and fifth most populous census statistical areas (Greater Los Angeles Area and San Francisco Bay Area, respectively), and eight of the nation's 50 most populated cities (Los Angeles, San Diego, San Jose, San Francisco, Fresno, Sacramento, Long Beach, and Oakland). Sacramento is the state capital, and has been since 1854. What is now California was first settled by various Native American tribes before being explored by a number of European expeditions throughout the 16th and 17th centuries. It was then claimed by the Spanish Empire as part of Alta California in the larger territory of New Spain. Alta California became a part of Mexico in 1821 following its successful war for independence, but would later be ceded to the United States in 1848 after the Mexican-American War. The western portion of Alta California was soon organized as the State of California, which was admitted as the 31st state on September 9, 1850. The California Gold Rush starting in 1848 led to dramatic social and demographic change, with large-scale immigration from the east and abroad with an accompanying economic boom. California's diverse geography ranges from the Pacific Coast in the west, to the Sierra Nevada in the east – from the Redwood–Douglas fir forests of the northwest, to the Mojave Desert areas in the southeast. The center of the state is dominated by the Central Valley, a major agricultural area. California contains both the highest and lowest points in the contiguous United States (Mount Whitney and Death Valley), and has the 3rd longest coastline of all states (after Alaska and Florida). Earthquakes are a common occurrence because of the state's location along the Pacific Ring of Fire: about 37,000 are recorded annually, but most are too small to feel. At least half of the fruit produced in the United States is now cultivated in California, and the state also leads in the production of vegetables. Other important contributors to the state's economy include aerospace, education, manufacturing, and high-tech industry. If it were a country, California would be the 8th or 9th largest economy in the world and the 34th most populous.

Chief Justice

The Chief Justice is the name for the presiding member of a supreme court in many countries with a justice system based on English common law, such as the Supreme Court of Canada, the Constitutional Court of South Africa, the Court of Final Appeal of Hong Kong, the Supreme Court of India, the Supreme Court of Pakistan, the Supreme Court of Nepal, the Supreme Court of Ireland, the

Supreme Court of New Zealand, the High Court of Australia, the Supreme Court of the United States, and provincial or state supreme courts. The situation is slightly different in the three legal jurisdictions within the United Kingdom. The courts of England and Wales are headed by the Lord Chief Justice of England and Wales; in Northern Ireland's courts, the equivalent position is the Lord Chief Justice of Northern Ireland and in Scottish courts, the equivalent is the Lord President of the Court of Session. These three judges are not, though, part of the Supreme Court of the United Kingdom, which operates across all three jurisdictions and is headed by the President of the Supreme Court of the United Kingdom. The Chief Justice can be selected in many ways, but, in many nations, the position is given to the most senior justice of the court, while, in the United States, it is often the President's most important political nomination, subject to approval by the United States Senate. Although the title of this top American jurist is, by statute, Chief Justice of the United States, the term "Chief Justice of the Supreme Court" is often used unofficially. In some courts, the Chief Justice has a different title, e.g. President of the Supreme Court. In other courts, the title of Chief Justice is used, but the court has a different name, e.g. the Supreme Court of Judicature in colonial (British) Ceylon, and the Maryland Court of Appeals (in the US state of Maryland).

Circuit Court of Appeals

The United States Court of Appeals for the Ninth Circuit (in case citations, 9th Cir.) is a U.S. Federal court with appellate jurisdiction over the district courts in the following districts: District of Alaska District of Arizona Central District of California Eastern District of California Northern District of California Southern District of California District of Hawaii District of Idaho District of Montana District of Nevada District of Oregon Eastern District of Washington Western District of Washington It also has appellate jurisdiction over the following territorial courts: District of Guam District of the Northern Mariana Islands Headquartered in San Francisco, California, the Ninth Circuit is by far the largest of the thirteen courts of appeals, with 29 active judgeships. The court's regular meeting places are Seattle at the William K. Nakamura Courthouse, Portland at the Pioneer Courthouse, San Francisco at the James R. Browning U.S. Court of Appeals Building, and Pasadena at the Richard H. Chambers U.S. Court of Appeals. Panels of the court occasionally travel to hear cases in other locations within the circuit. Although the judges travel around the circuit, the court arranges its hearings so that cases from the northern region of the circuit are heard in Seattle or Portland, cases from southern California are heard in Pasadena, and cases from northern California, Nevada, Arizona, and Hawaii are heard in San Francisco. For lawyers who must come and present their cases to the court in person, this administrative grouping of cases helps to reduce the time and cost of travel.

civil rights

Civil and political rights are a class of rights that protect individuals' freedom from infringement by governments, social organizations, and private individuals, and which ensure one's ability to participate in the civil and political life of the society and state without discrimination or repression. Civil rights include the ensuring of peoples' physical and mental integrity, life and safety; protection from discrimination on grounds such as race, gender, national origin, colour, sexual orientation, ethnicity, religion, or disability; and individual rights such as privacy, the freedoms of thought and conscience, speech and expression, religion, the press, assembly and movement. Political rights include natural justice (procedural fairness) in law, such as the rights of the accused, including the right to a fair trial; due process; the right to seek redress or a legal remedy; and rights of participation in civil society and politics such as freedom of association, the right to assemble, the right to petition, the right of self-defense, and the right to vote. Civil and political rights form the original and main part of international human rights. They comprise the first portion of the 1948 Universal Declaration of Human Rights (with economic, social and cultural rights comprising the second portion). The theory of three generations of human rights considers this group of rights to be "first-generation rights", and the theory of negative and positive rights considers them to be generally negative rights.

commander

Commander is a naval rank which is also sometimes used as a military title depending on the individual customs of a given military service. Commander is also used as a rank or title in some organizations outside of the armed forces, particularly in police and law enforcement.

Commander in Chief

A commander-in-chief is the person or body that exercises supreme operational command and control of a nation's military forces or significant elements of those forces. In the latter case, the force element is those forces within a particular region, or associated by function. As a practical term, it refers to military competencies that reside in a nation-state's executive leadership—either a head of state, a head of government, a minister of defence, a national cabinet, or some other collegial body. Often, a given country's commander-in-chief (if held by an official) need not be or have been a commissioned officer or even a veteran. This follows the principle of civilian control of the military. The role of commander-in-chief derives from the Latin, imperator. Imperatores of the Roman Republic and Roman Empire possessed imperium (command) powers. In its modern use, the term first applied to King Charles I of England in 1639. A nation's head of state (monarchical or republican) usually holds the nominal position of commander-in-chief, even if effective executive power is held by a separate head of government. In a parliamentary system, the executive branch is ultimately dependent upon the will of the legislature; although the legislature does not issue orders directly to the armed forces and therefore does not control the military in any operational sense. Governors-general and colonial governors are also often appointed commander-in-chief of the military forces within their territory. A commander-in-chief is sometimes referred to as Supreme Commander, which is sometimes used as a specific term. The term is also used for military officers who hold such power and authority, not always through dictatorship, and as a subordinate (usually) to a head of state (see Generalissimo). The term is also used for officers that hold authority over individual branches or within a theatre of operations.

Commerce Commission

The Commerce Commission is a New Zealand government agency charged with enforcing legislation that promotes competition in the country's markets and prohibits misleading and deceptive conduct by traders. It is an independent, quasi-judicial body, established under the Commerce Act 1986. The purpose of the Act is to promote competition in New Zealand's market economy. It prohibits conducts that restricts competition (restrictive trade practices) and the purchase of a business's shares or assets if that purchase leads to a substantial lessening of competition in the market.

concentration camps

Internment is the imprisonment or confinement of people, commonly in large groups, without trial. Collins English dictionary defines internment as "the act of interning or state of being interned, esp of enemy citizens in wartime or of terrorism suspects". Thus, while it can simply mean imprisonment, it tends to refer to preventative confinement rather than confinement after having been convicted of some crime. Use of these terms is subject to debate and political sensitivities. Interned persons may be held at prisons, or at facilities known as internment camps. In certain contexts these may be known, either officially or pejoratively, as concentration camps. Internment also refers to the practice of neutral countries in time of war in detaining belligerent armed forces and equipment in their territories under the Hague Convention of 1907. The Universal Declaration of Human Rights restricts the use of internment. Article 9 states that "No one shall be subjected to arbitrary arrest, detention or exile."

Congress

A congress is a formal meeting of the representatives of different nations, constituent states, independent organizations (such as trade unions), or groups. The term was chosen for the Continental Congress to emphasize the status of each colony represented there as a self-governing unit. Subsequent to the use of congress by the U.S. legislature, the term has been adopted by many states within unions, and by unitary nation-states in the Americas, to refer to their legislatures.

constitutional law

Constitutional law is the body of law which defines the relationship of different entities within a state, namely, the executive, the legislature, and the judiciary. Not all nation states have codified constitutions, though all such states have a jus commune, or law of the land, that may consist of a variety of imperative and consensual rules. These may include customary law, conventions, statutory law, judge-made law, or international rules and norms.

constitutionalrights

A constitutional right is a legal right of its citizens (and possibly others within its jurisdiction) protected by a sovereignty's constitution.

constitutional rights

A constitutional right is a legal right of its citizens (and possibly others within its jurisdiction) protected by a sovereignty's constitution.

Constitutionalrights

A constitutional right is a legal right of its citizens (and possibly others within its jurisdiction) protected by a sovereignty's constitution.

Court

A court is a tribunal, often a governmental institution, with the authority to adjudicate legal disputes between parties and carry out the administration of justice in civil, criminal, and administrative matters in accordance with the rule of law. In both common law and civil law legal systems, courts are the central means for dispute resolution, and it is generally understood that all persons have an ability to bring their claims before a court. Similarly, the rights of those accused of a crime include the right to present a defense before a court. The system of courts that interprets and applies the law is collectively known as the judiciary. The place where a court sits is known as a venue. The room where court proceedings occur is known as a courtroom, and the building as a courthouse; court facilities range from simple and very small facilities in rural communities to large buildings in cities. The practical authority given to the court is known as its jurisdiction (Latin jus dicere) – the court's power to decide certain kinds of questions or petitions put to it. According to William Blackstone's Commentaries on the Laws of England, a court is constituted by a minimum of three parties: the actor or plaintiff, who complains of an injury done; the reus or defendant, who is called upon to make satisfaction for it, and the judex or judicial power, which is to examine the truth of the fact, to determine the law arising upon that fact, and, if any injury appears to have been done, to ascertain and by its officers to apply a legal remedy. It is also usual in the superior courts to have attorneys, and advocates or counsel, as assistants, though, often, courts consist of additional attorneys, bailiffs, reporters, and perhaps a jury. The term "the court" is also used to refer to the presiding officer or officials, usually one or more judges. The judge or panel of judges may also be collectively referred to as "the bench" (in contrast to attorneys and barristers, collectively referred to as "the bar"). In the United States, and other common law jurisdictions, the term "court" (in the case of U.S. federal courts) by law is used to describe the judge himself or herself. In the United States, the legal authority of a court to take action is based on personal jurisdiction, subject-matter jurisdiction, and venue over the parties to the litigation.

District Court

District courts are a category of courts which exists in several nations. These include:

Executive Order

United States Presidents issue executive orders to help officers and agencies of the executive branch manage the operations within the federal government itself. Executive orders have the full force of law when they take authority from a legislative power which grants its power directly to the Executive by the Constitution, or are made in pursuance of certain Acts of Congress that explicitly delegate to the President some degree of discretionary power (delegated legislation). Like both legislative statutes and regulations promulgated by government agencies, executive orders are subject to judicial review, and may be struck down if deemed by the courts to be unsupported by statute or the Constitution. Major policy initiatives require approval by the legislative branch, but executive orders have significant influence over the internal affairs of government, deciding how and to what degree legislation will be enforced, dealing with emergencies, waging 72-hour length strikes on enemies, and in general fine-tuning policy choices in the implementation of broad statutes.

Federal Bureau of Investigation

The Federal Bureau of Investigation (FBI) is a governmental agency belonging to the United States Department of Justice that serves as both a federal criminal investigative organization and an internal intelligence agency. The FBI is the lead U.S. counterterrorism agency and the lead U.S. counterintelligence agency. It is the USA's security service, and is a component agency of the U.S. Intelligence Community. Also, it is the government agency responsible for investigating crimes on sovereign Native American reservations in the United States under the Major Crimes Act. The FBI has investigative jurisdiction over violations of more than 200 categories of federal crime. The bureau was established in 1908 as the Bureau of Investigation (BOI). Its name was changed to the Federal Bureau of Investigation (FBI) in 1935. The FBI headquarters is the J. Edgar Hoover Building, located in Washington, D.C. The bureau has fifty-six field offices located in major cities throughout the United States, and more than 400 resident agencies in lesser cities and areas across the nation. More than 50 international offices called "legal attachés" exist in U.S. embassies and consulates general worldwide.

General DeWitt

John Lesesne DeWitt (January 9, 1880-June 20, 1962) was a general in the United States Army, best known for his vocal support of the internment of Japanese-Americans and his role supervising the combat operations in the Aleutian Islands, some of which had been invaded by Japanese forces during World War II. General DeWitt believed that Japanese and Japanese Americans in California, Oregon, and Washington could be conspiring against the American war effort, and recommended they be removed from coastal areas. President Franklin D. Roosevelt agreed, and issued Executive Order 9066, which directed the forced removal of men, women and children of Japanese ancestry to federal internment camps. Dewitt issued military proclamations to carry out the order, incarcerating 110,000 Japanese men, women and children, 62% of whom were American-born citizens.

Government

A government is the system by which a state or community is governed. In the Commonwealth of Nations, the word government is also used more narrowly to refer to the collective group of people that exercises executive authority in a state. This usage is analogous to what is called an "administration" in American English. Furthermore, government is occasionally used in English as a synonym for governance. In the case of its broad associative definition, government normally consists of legislators, administrators, and arbitrators. Government is the means by which state policy is enforced, as well as the mechanism for determining the policy of the state. A form of government, or form of state governance, refers to the set of political systems and institutions that make up the organisation of a specific government. Government of any kind currently affects every human activity in many important ways. For this reason, political scientists generally argue that government should not be studied by itself; but should be studied along with anthropology, economics, history, philosophy, science, and sociology.

Hirabayashi

Hirabayashi is a Japanese surname. It may refer to: Gordon Hirabayashi (1918–2012), American sociologist James Hirabayashi, American academic (San Francisco State University, first dean of the first school of ethnic studies Jay Hirabayashi, Japanese Canadian dancer, co-founder of Kokoro Dance Keith Hirabayashi Cooke, American martial artist Keith Cooke Morito Hirabayashi, commander of one of five major Japanese forces in the Central Hupei Operation Hirabayashi Taiko (1905-1972), Japanese author

House

A house is a building that functions as a home for humans or other creatures, ranging from simple dwellings such as rudimentary huts of nomadic tribes to complex structures composed of many systems. The social unit that lives in a house is known as a household. Most commonly, a household is a family unit of some kind, although households may also be other social groups or individuals.

House of Representatives

House of Representatives is the name of legislative bodies in many countries and sub-national entities. In many countries, the House of Representatives is the lower house of a bicameral legislature, with the corresponding upper house often called a "Senate". In some countries, the House of Representatives is the sole chamber of a unicameral legislature. The functioning of a house of representatives can vary greatly from country to country, and depends on whether a country has a parliamentary or a presidential system. Members of a House of Representatives are typically apportioned according to population rather than geography.

intelligence services

An intelligence agency is a government agency responsible for the collection, analysis, and exploitation of information and intelligence in support of law enforcement, national security, defence and foreign policy objectives. Means of information gathering are both overt and covert and may include espionage, communication interception, cryptanalysis, cooperation with other institutions, and evaluation of public sources. The assembly and propagation of this information is known as intelligence analysis or intelligence assessment. Intelligence agencies can provide the following services for their national governments. Provision of analysis in areas relevant to national security; give early warning of impending crises; serve national and international crisis management by helping to discern the intentions of current or potential opponents; inform national defence planning and military operations; protect sensitive information secrets, both of their own sources and activities, and those of other state agencies; may act covertly to influence the outcome of events in favour of national interests, or influence international security; and Defence against the efforts of other national intelligence agencies (counter-intelligence). There is a distinction between "security intelligence" and "foreign intelligence". Security intelligence pertains to domestic threats (e.g. terrorism, espionage). Foreign intelligence involves information collection relating to the political, or economic activities of foreign states. Some agencies have been involved in assassination, arms trafficking, coups d'état, and the placement of misinformation (propaganda) as well as other covert operations, in order to support their own or their governments' interests.

Interstate Commerce Commission

The Interstate Commerce Commission (ICC) was a regulatory agency in the United States created by the Interstate Commerce Act of 1887. The agency's original purpose was to regulate railroads (and later trucking) to ensure fair rates, to eliminate rate discrimination, and to regulate other aspects of common carriers, including interstate bus lines and telephone companies. Congress expanded ICC authority to regulate other modes of commerce beginning in 1906. The agency was abolished in 1995, and its remaining functions were transferred to the Surface Transportation Board. The Commission's five members were appointed by the President of the United States with the consent of the United States Senate; the commission was authorized to investigate violations of the Act and order the cessation of wrongdoing. However, in its early years, ICC orders required an order by a federal court to become effective. The Commission was the first independent regulatory body (or so-called Fourth Branch), as well as the first agency to regulate big business in the U.S.

Japan

Japan /d ə pæn/ (Japanese: Nippon or Nihon; formally Nippon-koku or Nihon-koku, literally "[the] State of Japan") is an island nation in East Asia. Located in the Pacific Ocean, it lies to the east of the Sea of Japan, China, North Korea, South Korea and Russia, stretching from the Sea of Okhotsk in the north to the East China Sea and Taiwan in the south. The characters that make up Japan's name mean "sun-origin", which is why Japan is often referred to as the "Land of the Rising Sun". Japan is a stratovolcanic archipelago of 6,852 islands. The four largest islands are Honshu, Hokkaido, Kyushu, and Shikoku, which together comprise about ninety-seven percent of Japan's land area. Japan has the world's tenth-largest population, with over 126 million people. Honshū's Greater Tokyo Area, which includes the de facto capital of Tokyo and several surrounding prefectures, is the largest metropolitan area in the world, with over 30 million residents. Archaeological research indicates that people lived in Japan as early as the Upper Paleolithic period. The first written mention of Japan is in Chinese history texts from the 1st century AD. Influence from other regions, mainly China, followed by periods of isolation, particularly from Western European influence, has characterized Japan's history. From the 12th century until 1868, Japan was ruled by successive feudal military shoguns in the name of the Emperor. Japan entered into a long period of isolation in the early 17th century, which was only ended in 1853 when a United States fleet pressured Japan to open to the West. Nearly two decades of internal conflict and insurrection followed before the Meiji Emperor was restored as head of state in 1868 and the Empire of Japan was proclaimed, with the Emperor as a divine symbol of the nation. In the late 19th and early 20th centuries, victories in the First Sino-Japanese War, the Russo-Japanese War and World War I allowed Japan to expand its empire during a period of increasing militarism. The Second Sino-Japanese War of 1937 expanded into part of World War II in 1941, which came to an end in 1945 following the atomic bombings of Hiroshima and Nagasaki. Since adopting its revised constitution in 1947, Japan has maintained a unitary constitutional monarchy with an emperor and an elected legislature called the Diet. A major economic power, Japan is a developed country and has the world's third-largest economy by nominal GDP and the world's fourth-largest economy by purchasing power parity. It is also the world's fourth-largest exporter and fourth-largest importer. Although Japan has officially renounced its right to declare war, it maintains a modern military with the world's eighth largest military budget, used for self-defense and peacekeeping roles. Japan ranks high in metrics of prosperity such as the Human Development Index, with the Japanese population enjoying the highest life expectancy of any country in the world and the infant mortality rate being the third lowest globally.

Judge Cardozo

Kim McLane Wardlaw (born July 2, 1954) is a federal judge on the United States Court of Appeals for the Ninth Circuit, with chambers in Pasadena, California.

Korematsu

Fred Toyosaburo Korematsu (, Korematsu Toyosaburō, January 30, 1919 – March 30, 2005) was one of the many Japanese-American citizens living on the West Coast of the United States at the onset of World War II. Shortly after the Imperial Japanese Navy attacked Pearl Harbor, President Franklin D. Roosevelt issued Executive Order 9066, authorizing the Secretary of War and his military commanders to remove all individuals of Japanese ancestry from designated "military areas" and place them in internment camps in what is known as the Japanese American internment. When such orders were issued for the West Coast, Korematsu instead became a fugitive. The legality of the internment order was upheld by the United States Supreme Court in Korematsu v. United States, but Korematsu's conviction was overturned decades later after the disclosure of new evidence challenging the necessity of the internment, evidence which had been withheld from the courts by the U.S. government during the war. To commemorate his journey as a civil rights activist, the "Fred Korematsu Day of Civil Liberties and the Constitution" was observed for first time on January 30, 2011, by the state of California, and first such commemoration for an Asian American in the US.

Lieutenant General DeWitt

Hirabayashi v. United States, 320 U.S. 81 (1943),[1] was a case in which the United States Supreme Court held that the application of curfews against members of a minority group were constitutional when the nation was at war with the country from which that group originated. The case arose out of the issuance of Executive Order 9066 following the December 1941 attack on Pearl Harbor and the U.S. entry into World War II. President Franklin Roosevelt had authorized military commanders to secure areas from which "any or all persons may be excluded," and Japanese Americans were subject to a curfew and other restrictions before being removed to internment camps. The plaintiff, Gordon Hirabayashi, was convicted of violating the curfew and had appealed to the Supreme Court. Yasui v. United States was a companion case decided the same day. Both convictions were overturned in coram nobis proceedings in the 1980s.

martial law

Martial law is the imposition of the highest-ranking military officer as the military governor or as the head of the government, thus removing all power from the previous executive, legislative, and judicial branches of government. It is usually imposed temporarily when the government or civilian authorities fail to function effectively (e.g., maintain order and security, or provide essential services). Martial law can be used by governments to enforce their rule over the public. Such incidents may occur after a coup d'état (such as Thailand in 2006 and 2014); when threatened by popular protest (China, Tiananmen Square protests of 1989); to suppress political opposition (Poland in 1981); or to stabilize insurrections or perceived insurrections (Canada, The October Crisis of 1970). Martial law may be declared in cases of major natural disasters; however, most countries use a different legal construct, such as a state of emergency. Martial law has also been imposed during conflicts and in cases of occupations, where the absence of any other civil government provides for an unstable population. Examples of this form of military rule include post World War II reconstruction in Germany and Japan as well as the southern reconstruction following the U.S. Civil War. Typically, the imposition of martial law accompanies curfews, the suspension of civil law, civil rights, habeas corpus, and the application or extension of military law or military justice to civilians. Civilians defying martial law may be subjected to military tribunal (court-martial).

McWilliams

McWilliams is a surname. Notable people with the surname include: Alfred McWilliams (b. 1844, d. unknown), Canadian politician from Prince Edward Island Bill McWilliams (1910–1997), American professional baseball player Brendan McWilliams (1944–2007), Irish meteorologist and science writer Carey McWilliams (1905–1980), American author, editor, and lawyer Carey McWilliams (b. 1973), American author, marksman, and skydiver Caroline McWilliams (b. 1945), American television actress; former wife of Michael Keaton Christopher 'Crip' McWilliams (1963–2008), Irish nationalist; convicted of the murder of the LVF leader Billy Wright Cynthia Kaye McWilliams (contemporary), American actress David McWilliams (contemporary), American college football coach David McWilliams (1945–2002), Northern Irish singer, songwriter, and guitarist David McWilliams (b. 1966), Irish economist, commentator, and author Derek McWilliams (b. 1966), Scottish professional football player Edmund McWilliams (contemporary), American diplomat and ambassador Eric McWilliams (b. 1950), American professional basketball player Fleming McWilliams (contemporary), American singer and songwriter Jackie McWilliams (b. 1964), Irish Olympic field hockey player Jeremy McWilliams (b. 1964), Irish motorcycle road racer Joe McWilliams (1904–1996), American inventor, industrial engineer, and nationalist John D. McWilliams (1891–1975), American politician from Connecticut; U.S. Representative 1943–45 Johnny McWilliams (b. 1972), American professional football player Larry McWilliams (b. 1954), American professional baseball player Monica McWilliams (b. 1954), Northern Ireland academic and politician Peter McWilliams (1949–2000), American marijuana activist and writer Rhys McWilliams (b. 1985), English professional ice hockey player Roland Fairbairn McWilliams (1874–1957), Canadian politician from Manitoba Shorty McWilliams (1926–1997), American football player Taj McWilliams-Franklin (b. 1970), American professional women's basketball player William McWilliams (1856–1929), Australian politician from Tasmania Wilson Carey McWilliams (1933–2005), American political scientist and writer

Military Area

A restricted military area or military out-of-bounds area is an area under military jurisdiction where special security measures are used to prevent unauthorized entry.

Military Commander

The commanding officer (CO) is the officer in command of a military unit. Typically, the commanding officer has ultimate authority over the unit, and is usually given wide latitude to run the unit as he or she sees fit, within the bounds of military law. In this respect, commanding officers have significant responsibilities (for example, the use of force, finances, equipment, the Geneva Conventions), duties (to higher authority, mission effectiveness, duty of care to personnel), and powers (for example, discipline and punishment of personnel within certain limits of military law). In some countries, commanding officers may be of any commissioned rank. Usually, there are more officers than command positions available, and time spent in command is generally a key aspect of promotion, so the role of commanding officer is highly valued, and in theory, only goes to the best officers. The commanding officer is often assisted by an executive officer (XO) or second-in-command (2i/c), who handles personnel and day-to-day matters and a senior enlisted advisor. Larger units may also have staff officers responsible for various responsibilities.

MR. JUSTICE BLACK

Hugo Lafayette Black (February 27, 1886 – September 25, 1971) was an American politician and jurist. A member of the Democratic Party, Black represented Alabama in the United States Senate from 1927 to 1937, and served as an Associate Justice of the Supreme Court of the United States from 1937 to 1971. Black was nominated to the Supreme Court by President Franklin D. Roosevelt and confirmed by the Senate by a vote of 63 to 16. (6 Democratic Senators and 10 Republican Senators voted against him.) He was first of nine Roosevelt nominees to the Court, and he outlasted all except for William O. Douglas. Black is widely regarded as one of the most influential Supreme Court justices in the 20th century. The fifth longest-serving justice in Supreme Court history, Black is noted for his advocacy of a textualist reading of the United States Constitution and of the position that the liberties guaranteed in the Bill of Rights were imposed on the states ("incorporated") by the Fourteenth Amendment. During his political career, Black was regarded as a staunch supporter of liberal policies and civil liberties. However, Black consistently opposed the doctrine of substantive due process (the anti-New Deal Supreme Court cited this concept in such a way as to make it impossible for the government to enact legislation that interfered with the freedom of business owners) and believed that there was no basis in the words of the Constitution for a right to privacy, voting against finding one in Griswold v. Connecticut. Black endorsed Roosevelt in both the 1932 and 1936 US Presidential elections and was a staunch supporter of the New Deal.

National War Agencies

A news agency is an organization that gathers news reports and sells them to subscribing news organizations, such as newspapers, magazines, and radio and television broadcasters. A news agency may also be referred to as a wire service, newswire, or news service. There are many news agencies around the world, but four are global news agencies which have offices in most countries of the world and cover all areas of information: Agence France-Presse (formerly the Havas agency), Associated Press, Reuters and Agencia EFE. All four began with and continue to operate on a basic philosophy of providing a single objective news feed to all subscribers; they do not provide separate feeds for conservative or liberal newspapers. Fenby explains the philosophy: to achieve such wide acceptability, the agencies avoid overt partiality. Demonstrably correct information is their stock in trade. Traditionally, they report at a reduced level of responsibility, attributing their information to a spokesman, the press, or other sources. They avoid making judgments and steer clear of doubt and ambiguity. Though their founders did not use the word, objectivity is the philosophical basis for their enterprises – or failing that, widely acceptable neutrality.

New York Times

The New York Times (NYT) is an American daily newspaper, founded and continuously published in New York City since September 18, 1851, by The New York Times Company. It has won 114 Pulitzer Prizes, more than any other news organization. The paper's print version remains the largest metropolitan newspaper in the United States and second-largest newspaper overall, behind The Wall Street Journal. It is ranked 39th in the world by circulation. Following industry trends, its weekday circulation has fallen to fewer than one million daily since 1990. Nicknamed for years as "The Gray Lady", The New York Times is long regarded within the industry as a national "newspaper of record". It is owned by The New York Times Company. Arthur Ochs Sulzberger Jr., (whose family (Ochs-Sulzberger) has controlled the paper for five generations, since 1896), is both the paper's publisher and the company's chairman. Its international version, formerly the International Herald Tribune, is now called the International New York Times. The paper's motto, "All the News That's Fit to Print", appears in the upper left-hand corner of the front page. Its website has adapted it to "All the News That's Fit to Click". Since the mid-1970s, it has greatly expanded its lay-out and organization, adding special weekly sections on various topics supplementing the regular news, editorials, sports and features. Recently it has been organized into sections: News, Editorials/Opinions-Columns/"Op-Ed", "New York" (metropolitan), "Business", "Sports of The Times", "Arts", "Science", "Styles", "Home", and other features. On Sunday, it is supplemented by sections of "The Week in Review", "The New York Times Book Review" and "The New York Times Magazine" and recently "T", the Style magazine. "The Times" stayed with the "broadsheet" full page set-up (as some others have changed into a tabloid lay-out) and an eight-column format for several years after most papers switched to six, and was one of the last newspapers to adopt color photography, especially on the front page.

Oregon

Oregon (/ r ən/ ORR-ə-gən) is a state in the Pacific Northwest of the United States. It is bordered on its west by the Pacific Ocean, north by Washington, south by California, east by Idaho, and southeast by Nevada. The Columbia River delineates much of Oregon's northern boundary, the Snake River largely its eastern. Oregon's area was inhabited by many indigenous tribes before traders, explorers, and settlers arrived. An autonomous government was formed in Oregon Country in 1843, Oregon Territory was created in 1848, and Oregon became the 33rd state on February 14, 1859. It is the 9th largest and 27th most populous state. Its capital is Salem, third most populous of its cities. With 603,106 (2012 estimate) residents Portland ranks 1st in Oregon, and 28th in the U.S. Its metro population of 2,262,605 (2011 estimate) is 23rd. The Willamette River Valley in western Oregon is the state's most densely populated area, home to eight of the ten most populous cities. Oregon's landscape is diverse, with a windswept Pacific coastline, volcano studded Cascade Mountains, abundant waterfalls, dense evergreen forests, mixed forests, and deciduous forests at lower elevations, and high desert sprawling across much of its east all the way to the Great Basin. The tall Douglas firs and redwoods along its rainy west coast contrast with the lighter timbered and fire-prone pine and juniper forests covering portions to the east. Abundant alders in the west fix nitrogen for the conifers; aspen groves are common in the east. Stretching east from central Oregon are semi-arid shrublands, prairies, deserts, steppes, and meadows. At 11,249 feet (3,429 m) Mount Hood is the state high point, Crater Lake National Park its only national park.

Pacific Coast

A country's Pacific coast is the part of its coast bordering the Pacific Ocean.

Pearl Harbor

Pearl Harbor is a lagoon harbor on the island of Oahu, Hawaii, west of Honolulu. Much of the harbor and surrounding lands is a United States Navy deep-water naval base. It is also the headquarters of the United States Pacific Fleet. The attack on Pearl Harbor by the Empire of Japan on Sunday, December 7, 1941 brought the United States into World War II.

President

A president is the leader of a country or a division or part of a country, typically a republic, a democracy, or a dictatorship. The title "president" is sometimes used by extension for leaders of other groups. Etymologically, a president is one who presides (from Latin prae- "before" + sedere "to sit"; giving the term praeses). Originally, the term referred to the presiding officer of a ceremony or meeting (i.e., chairman), but today it most commonly refers to an executive official. Among other things, "President" today is a common title for the heads of state of most republics, whether popularly elected, chosen by the legislature or by a special electoral college.

Relocation Authority

The War Relocation Authority (WRA) was a United States government agency established to handle the internment, i.e. forced relocation and detention, of

Japanese Americans during World War II. It also operated the Fort Ontario Emergency Refugee Shelter in Oswego, New York, which was the only refugee camp set up in the United States for refugees from the Holocaust.

Relocation Center

Internment is the imprisonment or confinement of people, commonly in large groups, without trial. Collins English dictionary defines internment as "the act of interning or state of being interned, esp of enemy citizens in wartime or of terrorism suspects". Thus, while it can simply mean imprisonment, it tends to refer to preventative confinement rather than confinement after having been convicted of some crime. Use of these terms is subject to debate and political sensitivities. Interned persons may be held at prisons, or at facilities known as internment camps. In certain contexts these may be known, either officially or pejoratively, as concentration camps. Internment also refers to the practice of neutral countries in time of war in detaining belligerent armed forces and equipment in their territories under the Hague Convention of 1907. The Universal Declaration of Human Rights restricts the use of internment. Article 9 states that "No one shall be subjected to arbitrary arrest, detention or exile."

San Leandro

San Leandro is a suburban city in Alameda County, California, United States. The population was 86,869 in 2014. It is located on the eastern shore of San Francisco Bay, between Oakland to the northwest and Hayward to the southeast.

Secretary

A secretary, personal assistant, or administrative assistant is a person whose work consists of supporting management, including executives, using a variety of project management, communication, or organizational skills. These functions may be entirely carried out to assist one other employee or may be for the benefit of more than one. In other situations a secretary is an officer of a society or organization who deals with correspondence, admits new members, and organizes official meetings and events.

six months

"Six Months in a Leaky Boat" is a single from New Zealand art rock group Split Enz's album Time and Tide. It was written by Tim Finn and released as a single in 1982. The song is a reference to the time it took pioneers to sail to Australia and New Zealand (hence the reference to "the tyranny of distance" - a history by Geoffrey Blainey), and a metaphor that refers to lead singer Tim Finn's nervous breakdown. The song was "discouraged from airplay" in Britain during the Falklands crisis by the BBC for reasons of morale - it was thought that references to leaky boats was not appropriate during the naval action in the war.

United States

The United States of America (USA or U.S.A.), commonly referred to as the United States (US or U.S.), America, and sometimes the States, is a federal republic consisting of 50 states and a federal district. The 48 contiguous states and Washington, D.C., are in central North America between Canada and Mexico. The state of Alaska is the northwestern part of North America and the state of Hawaii is an archipelago in the mid-Pacific. The country also has five populated and nine unpopulated territories in the Pacific and the Caribbean. At 3.80 million square miles (9.85 million km2) and with around 318 million people, the United States is the world's third- or fourth-largest country by total area and third-largest by population. It is one of the world's most ethnically diverse and multicultural nations, the product of large-scale immigration from many countries. The geography and climate of the United States is also extremely diverse, and it is home to a wide variety of wildlife. Paleo-Indians migrated from Eurasia to what is now the U.S. mainland around 15,000 years ago, with European colonization beginning in the 16th century. The United States emerged from 13 British colonies located along the Atlantic seaboard. Disputes between Great Britain and these colonies led to the American Revolution. On July 4, 1776, as the colonies were fighting Great Britain in the American Revolutionary War, delegates from the 13 colonies unanimously issued the Declaration of Independence. The war ended in 1783 with the recognition of independence of the United States from the Kingdom of Great Britain, and was the first successful war of independence against a European colonial empire. The current Constitution was adopted on September 17, 1787. The first ten amendments, collectively named the Bill of Rights, were ratified in 1791 and designed to guarantee many fundamental civil rights and freedoms. Driven by the doctrine of manifest destiny, the United States embarked on a vigorous expansion across North America throughout the 19th century. This involved displacing native tribes, acquiring new territories, and gradually admitting new states. During the second half of the 19th century, the American Civil War ended legal slavery in the country. By the end of that century, the United States extended into the Pacific Ocean, and its economy began to soar. The Spanish–American War and World War I confirmed the country's status as a global military power. The United States emerged from World War II as a global superpower, the first country to develop nuclear weapons, the only country to use them in warfare, and as a permanent member of the United Nations Security Council. The end of the Cold War and the dissolution of the Soviet Union left the United States as the sole superpower. The United States is a developed country and has the world's largest national economy. The economy is fueled by an abundance of natural resources and high worker productivity. While the U.S. economy is considered post-industrial, it continues to be one of the world's largest manufacturers. The country accounts for 37% of global military spending, being the world's foremost economic and military power, a prominent political and cultural force, and a leader in scientific research and technological innovations.

U.S. Army

The United States Army (USA) is the largest branch of the United States Armed Forces that performs land-based military operations. It is also the largest overall and oldest established branch of the U.S. military, and is one of seven U.S. uniformed services. The modern army has its roots in the Continental Army which was formed on 14 June 1775, to meet the demands of the American Revolutionary War before the establishment of the United States. The Congress of the Confederation officially created the United States Army on 3 June 1784 after the end of the Revolutionary War to replace the disbanded Continental Army. The army considers itself to be descended from the Continental Army and thus dates its inception from the origins of that force. The primary mission of the army is "to fight and win our Nation's wars by providing prompt, sustained land dominance across the full range of military operations and spectrum of conflict in support of combatant commanders." The army is a military service within the Department of the Army, one of the three military departments of the Department of Defense. The army is headed by the Secretary of the Army, and the top military officer in the department is the Chief of Staff of the Army. The highest ranking army officer is currently the Chairman of the Joint Chiefs of Staff. During fiscal year 2011, the Regular Army reported a strength of 546,057 soldiers; the Army National Guard (ARNG) reported 358,078 and the United States Army Reserve (USAR) reported 201,166 putting the combined component strength total at 1,105,301 soldiers. ˆ Wright, Jr., Robert K. (1983). The Continental Army (Army Lineage Series). Washington, DC: Center of Military History, United States Army. ISBN 9780160019319. OCLC 8806011. ˆ Maass, John R. "June 14th: The Birthday of the U.S. Army". U.S. Army Center of Military History. Retrieved 30 October 2013. ˆ a b Department of the Army, Deputy Chief of Staff (Human Resources/G-1), "Army Demographics – FY12 Army Profile" (demographics brochure) ˆ a b "14 June: The Birthday of the U.S. Army". United States Army Center of Military History. Retrieved 1 July 2011. an excerpt from Robert Wright, The Continental Army ˆ Library of Congress, Journals of the Continental Congress, Volume 27 ˆ "Army Birthdays". United States Army Center of Military History. 15 November 2004. Archived from the original on 20 April 2010. Retrieved Jun 2010 ˆ The United States

Army |Organization

www.ingramcontent.com/pod-product-compliance
Lightning Source LLC
Chambersburg PA
CBHW081903170526
45167CB00007B/3136